# ARMENIA 2016 HUMAN RIGHTS REPORT

## EXECUTIVE SUMMARY

Armenia's constitution provides for a republic with an elected head of state and a unicameral legislature, the National Assembly.  According to a constitutional referendum conducted in December 2015, the country is expected to transition gradually to a parliamentary republic by the end of the existing presidential term in 2018.  The Republican Party of Armenia (RPA) held a majority of seats in the National Assembly and, with President Serzh Sargsyan as leader, continued to dominate the country's political scene.  The country had a presidential election in 2013 and legislative elections in 2012.  The Organization for Security and Cooperation in Europe (OSCE) described the presidential election as well administered but with shortcomings, including an uneven playing field, serious election-day violations, and concerns regarding the integrity of the electoral process.  Similar flaws marred the 2012 National Assembly elections and the 2015 constitutional referendum.

Civilian authorities maintained effective control over the security forces.

On July 17, the armed group Sasna Tsrer stormed and occupied a police compound in Yerevan, taking police hostages.  During the two-week standoff that followed, Sasna Tsrer took additional police and medical personnel hostage, demanding political changes.  Group members allegedly killed three police officers during the incident.  During the standoff, numerous protests and demonstrations in support of Sasna Tsrer took place in Yerevan and other parts of the country.  Law enforcement officers engaged in illegal detentions, disproportionate and excessive use of force toward peaceful demonstrators, abusive treatment of journalists, and other serious human rights abuses, especially on the night of July 29, when police charged crowds supporting Sasna Tsrer's political demands.  While police suspended or applied disciplinary measures against more than a dozen officers, these measures did not adequately provide for accountability for the widespread abuses.

The most significant human rights problems during the year were law enforcement impunity; officials' use of government resources to maintain the political dominance of the ruling RPA combined with the use of economic and political power by the country's elite to enrich supporters and corrupt the law enforcement and judicial systems; and limited judicial independence.

Other reported problems included suspicious deaths in the military under noncombat conditions; bullying and mistreatment of conscripts by officers and fellow soldiers; allegations of abusive police behavior during arrest and interrogation; and harsh and overcrowded prison conditions. Arbitrary arrests and lengthy pretrial detention with a lack of transparency for the reasons for detention, a distrust of the veracity of testimony, unclear criteria for release, and an uneven application of rights such as family visitation for detainees occurred. Trials were often lengthy, and courts failed to enforce laws providing for fair trials. Inadequate law enforcement regarding violations of privacy and unlawful searches remained problems. Print and broadcast media lacked diversity of political opinion, and most television outlets reflected government views. Self-censorship was a problem. Police reportedly targeted journalists at citizens' protests. The politicization of both academic institutions and student activities inhibited academic freedom. Respect for freedom of assembly worsened. Authorities restricted freedom to participate in the political process and political pluralism. Government restrictions affected some minority religious groups, and members of religious minorities suffered from societal discrimination. Domestic violence remained a problem. An imbalance in the birth ratio of boys to girls pointed to gender-biased sex selection. Persons with disabilities experienced widespread discrimination. Lesbian, gay, bisexual, transgender, and intersex (LGBTI) persons experienced official abuse and discrimination as well as societal violence and discrimination. Society stigmatized persons with HIV/AIDS. The government limited workers' rights and weakly enforced labor laws.

The government conducted only cursory investigations into reports of abuses by officials. Law enforcement officers often committed abuses with impunity, at times under direct orders from law enforcement chiefs. Authorities did not hold anyone accountable for the 10 deaths that occurred following postelection clashes in 2008.

**Section 1. Respect for the Integrity of the Person, Including Freedom from:**

**a. Arbitrary Deprivation of Life and other Unlawful or Politically Motivated Killings**

Separatists, with Armenia's support, continued to control most of Nagorno-Karabakh and seven other Azerbaijani territories. The final status of Nagorno-Karabakh remained the subject of international mediation by the OSCE Minsk Group, cochaired by France, Russia, and the United States. There was an increase in violence along the Line of Contact and Armenian-Azerbaijan international border April 1-5.  The heavy clashes led to the highest death toll since the signing of the 1994 cease-fire agreement.  There were allegations of atrocities committed by the sides during the outbreak of violence.  The sides to the conflict also submitted complaints to the European Court of Human Rights accusing each other of committing atrocities during this period.

Noncombat deaths in the military remained a problem.  On April 26, the Investigative Committee of Armenia reported the death of Private Hovhannes Petrosyan, whose body was found with two gunshot wounds to the head in the trunk of a military truck.  Authorities initiated a criminal investigation into his death as an induced suicide.  According to press interviews, Petrosyan's family did not believe he committed suicide, claiming that his strained relations with an officer in his unit, whom Petrosyan reportedly prevented from stealing fuel from an official vehicle, led to his killing.  As of November no suspects had been arrested; the investigation continued at year's end.

Human rights observers asserted that authorities presented sanitized versions of reported incidents of noncombat deaths in the military and focused their follow-up investigations on reinforcing the initial versions.  In a March 2015 report on a wide range of human rights concerns, the commissioner for human rights of the Council of Europe, Nils Muiznieks, stated that he was "struck by the high level of distrust of the families of the victims and civil society in relation to such investigations."

On July 17, the armed group Sasna Tsrer occupied a police compound in Yerevan, demanding political changes.  During the two-week standoff that followed, Sasna Tsrer took police and medical personnel hostage for several days and allegedly killed three police officers during the incident:  one in the attack, another during the standoff, and a third from the injuries sustained in the attack (see section 1.c., 2.a., and 2.b.).

The Special Investigative Service (SIS) launched an investigation into the case based on articles of the criminal code proscribing seizure of buildings and illegal procurement and usage of weapons.  According to official information, SIS charged 62 persons (including 33 who carried out the armed attack), of whom 44 were detained as of October 25, and the investigation continued at year's end.  Authorities also charged group members with individual offenses such as murder and hostage taking.  During the attack, Sasna Tsrer allegedly killed police colonel Arthur Vanoyan, injured several others, and took several police officers as hostages, releasing them all by July 23.  On August 13, one of the injured police officers Gagik Mkrtchyan died from injuries sustained in the attack.  A Sasna Tsrer member, Armen Bilyan, was charged with Mkrtchyan's murder.  According to police, one of the attackers Smbat Barseghyan shot and killed police officer Yura Tepanosyan on July 30.  Barseghyan and the rest of the armed group denied their involvement in the killing of Tepanosyan.  From July 27 to 30, the group took medical personnel hostage.  There were no reports that any of the hostages, either police or medics, were subjected to any abuse or mistreatment while captured (also see sections 1.d., 2.a., and 2.b.).

## b. Disappearance

There were no reports of politically motivated disappearances.

## c. Torture and Other Cruel, Inhuman, or Degrading Treatment or Punishment

The law prohibits such practices.  Nevertheless, there were reports that members of the security forces regularly engaged in mistreating individuals in their custody.

Police abuse of suspects during their arrest, detention, and interrogation remained a significant problem.  According to human rights nongovernmental organizations (NGOs), most victims did not report abuses due to fear of retaliation.  Mistreatment occurred most often in police stations, which, unlike prisons and police detention facilities, were not subject to public monitoring.  According to the Public Observer's Group of Police Detention Facilities (POG), a coalition of NGOs that inspected police detention cells with permission of authorities, police used arrest itself as a form of punishment.  In his March 2015 report, the Council of Europe's human rights commissioner expressed concern regarding "persisting reports of torture and mistreatment by police and other law enforcement agencies-- often with the purpose of obtaining confessions--and the related problem of impunity."

During political protests related to Sasna Tsrer's July 17 seizure of the Erebuni police compound, there were numerous credible reports from local NGOs such as the Helsinki Committee of Armenia, Protection of Rights Without Borders, and the Helsinki Association of Human Rights that security forces engaged in cruel, inhuman, and degrading treatment of participants of assemblies, journalists, civic and political activists, and ordinary citizens (see sections 2.a. and 2.b.).

On July 29, police used excessive force against protesters, nonprotesters (including minors), and journalists in two locations in Yerevan near the occupied Erebuni police building.  While negotiations in Sari Tagh continued between some opposition leaders and the chief of Yerevan police, Ashot Karapetyan, the national chief of internal police troops, Levon Yeranosyan, gave a command, after which uniformed police threw grenades into the crowd, causing numerous shrapnel injuries, severe burns, and gas poisoning.  Simultaneously, armed civilians carrying improvised clubs charged the protesters and journalists covering the event, not allowing protesters a clear path to leave the area.  According to human rights NGOs and those observing the protests, while police warned the leaders that the crowd had to disperse, officials did not provide enough time for them to do so.  Instead, according to multiple accounts, law enforcement officers surrounded protesters with the apparent aim of punishing, injuring, and detaining them, thereby ending the protests.  In addition armed civilians, some of whom were later identified as members of the security details of the chief of police and of the neighborhood's National Assembly deputy physically, assaulted protesters and journalists.

According to official information, police detained more than 700 persons between July 17 and July 30 in connection with the standoff between police and the armed group Sasna Tsrer and associated protests.  In many instances individuals were detained simply for being at a certain location, regardless of whether they participated in a protest.  In some cases their rights to legal representation were not respected, and they were held in premises not intended for detentions and beyond the legal three-hour limit, without charges or access to a lawyer.  In some cases family members of activists were among those detained; when the activists appeared at police stations, police allegedly urged them to stop protesting or detained them for hours.  During this period, 51 police sought medical help for gunshot wounds and gas poisoning.

Following the July events, police suspended five officers for using excessive force and took disciplinary actions against 13 others for failure to prevent violent attacks on protesters and journalists during the events in Sari Tagh.  Four police officers, including Yerevan police chief Ashot Karapetyan, were later dismissed from their positions.  The SIS investigation of the criminal case into allegations of official abuse during the events continued at year's end.

On August 12, the NGO Helsinki Association for Human Rights published testimonies of victims of alleged police violence.  For example, Arsen Tadevosyan testified about his detention on the night of July 20, during which he stated police abuse resulted in a broken jaw and other injuries, and the refusal of the Shengavit police to provide him medical assistance.  The SIS considered him a victim in the investigation of police mistreatment of citizens.

On August 18, another NGO, the Helsinki Committee, published an extensive report detailing experiences of individuals detained by police after a July 17 rally. For example, a participant reported that police took him and at least 50 other rally participants to a gym in the Police Academy, where they were forced to walk between two rows of police who beat them.  While there, police with submachine guns periodically threatened the detainees, denied them access to water and toilets, and did not allow them to talk to other detainees.  During the entire period, they remained handcuffed.  Individuals who did not obey and tried to move or talk to other detainees, were taken to another room, beaten, and then brought back to the gym.  On July 18, activists Andranik Aslanyan, Davit Sanasaryan, and Artur Minasyan were reportedly beaten severely when detained.  Police continued to kick them while in transit to a police military unit, where they were abused further. Sanasaryan was kicked in the head until he lost consciousness and was later diagnosed with a concussion.

Although there were no reliable statistics on the extent of abuse in the military services, substandard living conditions, corruption, and commanders' lack of accountability contributed to mistreatment and injury of soldiers by their peers or superiors.  According to human rights organizations, a subculture based on "a criminal value system" undermined military discipline and resulted in a concept of "manly behavior" that overrode statutory rules.  According to the Ministry of Defense, this subculture led soldiers to underreport criminal behavior and abuse. While the military leadership recognized the problem and sought to overcome it, some observers maintained that certain military commanders regarded it, as well as violence towards conscripts in general, as an effective way to maintain discipline.

Drawing on interviews with 38 former military personnel for its 2015 annual report, the Helsinki Committee found that military police subjected soldiers in their custody to physical and other abuse, included beating, kicking, punching, hitting with rubber truncheons, and humiliating treatment.  Soldiers' families claimed that corrupt officials controlled many military units, and there were media reports during the year that the government conscripted soldiers with serious health conditions that should have disqualified them.

**Prison and Detention Center Conditions**

Prison conditions were marked by poor sanitation, inadequate medical care, and corruption; overcrowding in some facilities remained problems, and conditions in some cases were harsh and life threatening. Prisons generally lacked accommodations for inmates with disabilities.

<u>Physical Conditions</u>: Overcrowding was one of the most serious problems facing some prisons, especially the largest, Nubarashen Prison.

According to official data, 24 prisoners died during the first 10 months of the year, 17 due to illness and seven from suicide. According to human rights organizations, in addition to the poor physical condition of the facilities, an organized criminal structure that dominated prison life, hierarchical relations between inmates, and negligence in providing health care contributed to the death rate. Human rights observers also noted there were no proper investigations of these deaths.

On March 1, the government reported the suicide of Mkhitar Sargsyan, an inmate of the Nubarashen Prison. Sargsyan's wife, Satenik Hovsepyan, believed her husband was killed for refusing to take responsibility for the abuse of cellmate and civic activist Vardges Gaspari. On August 17, according to the NGO representing the victim's family, the Helsinki Citizens' Assembly Vanadzor (HCAV), the Investigative Committee suspended the investigation into Sargsyan's death due to failure to find those who induced him to suicide. According to the head of the HCAV, the investigation was insufficiently thorough to justify the conclusion that the case was a suicide rather than a homicide.

According to a report during the year by the NGO Protection of Rights without Borders on conditions at the Abovyan Prison, the facility did not meet the gender-specific needs of female inmates, such as appropriate medical care, sanitation, nutrition, and psychological services. Other problems included inedible food, insufficient restrooms and showers, limited access to running water, insufficient heating in winter, poor ventilation, no access to medical services, adequate medicine or exercise facilities, and limited job opportunities.

Most other prisons had similar problems. The Prison Monitoring Group (PMG) noted prison medical personnel lacked independence and had to obtain administrative approval to transfer an inmate to a hospital, record a physical injury in a prisoner's file, or perform similar actions. There was also at least one media report of medical neglect that led to a death of an inmate.

According to the PMG and other human rights activists, LGBTI individuals experienced the worst prison conditions.  They were frequent targets for discrimination, violence, and sexual abuse, and were forced by other inmates to perform degrading labor.  Prison administrators reinforced and condoned such treatment and held them in segregated cells, with terrible conditions.  According to the 2014 PMG report, physical violence and degrading treatment were common, with solitary confinement and beating with batons the most common forms of punishment.  The PMG noted that homosexual males, those associating with them, and inmates convicted of crimes such as rape were segregated from other inmates and forced to perform humiliating jobs and provide sexual services.

Administration:  Authorities did not conduct credible investigations nor take actions to address in a meaningful manner problems related to treatment of prisoners, relations between inmates, and widespread corruption.  No information was available on the adequacy of overall recordkeeping by prison authorities.  The early release program and release on medical grounds remained a matter of concern, due to systemic gaps in legislation and implementation.  Convicts and detainees did not always have reasonable access to visitors due to the lack of suitable space for visitations.  Heads of prisons and detention facilities used their discretion arbitrarily to deny prisoners and detainees visitation, contact with families, or the ability to receive periodicals.

Prisons did not have ombudsmen, and prisoners lacked effective mechanisms to report problems with their confinement.  Authorities did not always permit prisoners and detainees to submit uncensored appeals to authorities concerning credible allegations of inhuman conditions.

Independent Monitoring:  The government generally permitted domestic and international human rights groups, including the Council or Europe's Committee for the Prevention of Torture, to monitor prison and detention center conditions, and they did so regularly.  Their representatives could speak to prisoners privately.  The government permitted the International Committee of the Red Cross to visit both prisons and pretrial detention centers.

Prison authorities did not allow PMG monitors to visit detained members of the Sasna Tsrer group until December (see sections 1.d. and 2.b.).

**d. Arbitrary Arrest or Detention**

While the law prohibits arbitrary arrest and detention, police arbitrarily detained citizens, including participants in demonstrations.

**Role of the Police and Security Apparatus**

The national police force is responsible for internal security, while the National Security Service (NSS) is responsible for national security, intelligence activities, and border control.  The SIS is a separate agency specializing in preliminary investigation of cases involving suspected abuses by public officials.  The Investigative Committee is responsible for conducting pretrial investigations into criminal cases and incorporates investigative services.  The president appoints the heads of all these bodies.

Impunity was a problem, and no independent entity was dedicated exclusively to investigating police abuses.  According to human rights NGOs, law enforcement officers viewed themselves as defenders of authority rather than servants of the law and the public.  There were reports of impunity in connection with police use of excessive force during public protests in support of Sasna Tsrer's political demands (see section 1.c.).

The Ministry of Defense made efforts to improve discipline, including using the civilian legal system rather than administrative discipline to enforce regulations, training officers in human rights, and providing social, psychological, and legal training for military service.  In November 2015 the Ministry of Defense established the Center for Human Rights and Building Integrity, with a mandate to protect human rights, strengthen integrity, promote ethics, implement anticorruption policy, and make management changes, as well as coordinate with international organizations.

**Arrest Procedures and Treatment of Detainees**

Although the law requires law enforcement to obtain warrants or exercise reasonable suspicion in arrests, authorities on occasion detained and arrested suspects without warrants or reasonable suspicion.  By law an investigative body must either arrest or release individuals within three hours of taking them into custody.  Within 72 hours, the investigative body must release the arrested person or file charges and obtain a detention warrant from a judge.  Judges rarely denied police requests for detention warrants or reviewed police conduct during arrests.  According to the POG report, police did not keep accurate records and either backdated or failed to fill out protocols of detention and arrest.

The law requires police to inform detainees of the reasons for their detention or arrest as well as their right to remain silent and to make a telephone call. Bail was a legal option, but judges employed it rarely and selectively. In practice the judicial system and the law enforcement bodies placed the burden of proof on suspects to demonstrate they did not present a flight risk or would otherwise hamper the investigation, when determining the form of pretrial preventive measure.

Defendants were entitled to representation by an attorney from the moment of arrest. The law entitles detainees to public defenders if they are indigent. According to POG, few detainees were aware of their right to legal representation. Observers indicated police often avoided granting individuals their due-process rights by summoning and holding, rather than formally arresting, them, under the pretext that they were material witnesses rather than suspects. Police could thereby question individuals without giving them the benefit of a defense attorney.

Arbitrary Arrest: According to international organizations and human rights observers, police, NSS personnel, and border guards often detained or arrested individuals without a warrant. Human rights organizations stated such detentions were often a way to begin an investigation, with authorities hoping the suspect would confess and make further investigation unnecessary.

According to the preliminary findings of the fact-finding mission of the Civic Solidarity Platform conducted July 28 to August 1, there were cases in which plainclothes police seized protesters and took them to a police station. The report cited the testimony of Ara Petrosyan, who was walking in the neighborhood of the standoff when an unmarked car stopped and four plainclothes police forced him into the car without explanation, beat him, and then took him to the Erebuni Police Department. Police released him after several hours.

Pretrial Detention: Lengthy pretrial or preventive detention remained a chronic problem. According to official statistics, as of October 31, 9.6 percent of the prison population consisted of pretrial detainees, and an additional 22.7 percent were detainees whose trials were in progress or who were awaiting verdicts to enter into force. Some observers saw police use of excessive pretrial detention as a means of inducing defendants to confess or to reveal self-incriminating evidence. On October 20, the European Court of Human Rights (ECHR) in the case of *Ara Harutyunyan v. Armenia* ruled that the country violated the European Convention on Human Rights by failing to provide relevant and sufficient reasons for the applicant's detention.  The ECHR noted in its ruling that the use of stereotyped formulae when imposing and extending detention appeared to be a recurring problem in the country.

The overuse of detention applied also to juvenile offenders.  According to the Council of Europe's human rights commissioner, juveniles were especially vulnerable in the criminal justice system and were not protected from violations of their rights.

Although the law requires prosecutors to present a well-reasoned justification every two months for extending pretrial custody, judges routinely extended detention on unclear grounds.  Authorities generally complied with the six-month limit in ordinary cases and 12-month limit for serious crimes in terms of the total time in pretrial detention.  Once prosecutors forward their cases to court for trial, the law does not provide time limits on further detention but indicates only that a trial must be of "reasonable length."  Prosecutors regularly requested and received trial postponements from judges on the grounds needing more time to prepare.  Prosecutors tended to blame trial delays on defense lawyers and their requests for more time to prepare a defense.  Severely overburdened judicial dockets at all court levels also contributed to lengthy trials.

<u>Detainee's Ability to Challenge Lawfulness of Detention before a Court</u>: According to legal experts, suspects had no real opportunities to appeal the legality of their arrests.  In cases where the courts ruled on a pretrial detention, another court was unlikely to challenge its ruling.

## e. Denial of Fair Public Trial

Although the law provides for an independent judiciary, the judiciary did not generally exhibit independence.  Administrative courts, however, were relatively more independent than others.  There were reports the Court of Cassation dictated the outcome of all significant cases to lower-court judges.  According to observers, the Court of Cassation's control over judicial decisions remained an overarching problem affecting judicial independence.

In an October 27 ruling, the ECHR described the conduct of the chairman of the Court of Cassation in an eminent domain case as "lacking in the necessary detachment demanded by the principle of judicial neutrality" and stated he "raised an objectively justified fear that he lacked impartiality when deciding the applicant's case."

Judges remained subject to political pressure from every level of the executive branch, especially from law enforcement agencies, as well as from the judicial hierarchy. Lacking life tenure, they were vulnerable to dismissal and had no effective legal remedies if executive, legislative, or more senior judicial officials decided to punish them.

According to legal experts, the practice of investigators to request pretrial detentions that courts then felt compelled to satisfy, undermined judicial independence and reinforced the impression that courts were simply tools and that investigators actually determined the length of a detention. According to lawyers, past dismissals of certain judges for independent decisions still had a chilling effect on the judiciary as a whole.

In his March 2015 report, the Council of Europe's human rights commissioner, reflecting the concerns of human rights observers, stated that authorities used disciplinary proceedings unfairly against judges to influence their decisions or retaliate against them. He also noted the involvement of the minister of justice in disciplinary proceedings against judges, a practice incompatible with judicial independence.

Authorities generally complied with court orders.

Trials usually complied with procedural standards but were often unfair in substance, because many judges felt compelled to work with prosecutors to achieve convictions.

NGOs reported judges routinely ignored defendants' claims that their testimony was coerced through physical abuse. In his March 2015 report, the Council of Europe's human rights commissioner expressed serious concern about the reliance of courts on evidence that defendants claimed was obtained under duress, especially when such evidence was the basis for a conviction.

Human rights NGOs highlighted violations of the human rights of persons serving life sentences. According to these NGOs, individuals serving such sentences lacked the opportunity to have their sentences meaningfully reviewed by courts when changes in criminal law could possibly have resulted in less severe punishment. According to human rights groups, one of the greatest obstacles to justice for those serving life sentences was the court-ordered destruction of case files and evidence. This action deprived convicts of the opportunity to have their cases reviewed based on forensic analysis using technologies, such as DNA testing.

**Trial Procedures**

The constitution and laws provide for the right to a fair trial, but the judiciary lacked independence to enforce this right.

The law provides for presumption of innocence, but suspects usually did not enjoy this right. During trials authorities informed defendants in detail of the charges against them, and the law provided free language interpretation for non-Armenian speakers when necessary.

The law requires that most trials be public but permits exceptions, including in the interest of "morals," national security, and the "protection of the private lives of the participants." Defendants have the right to counsel of their own choosing, and the law requires the government to provide them with a public defender upon request. A shortage of defense lawyers sometimes led to denial of this right outside of Yerevan.

The law limits the defendant's right and time available to prepare a defense at the pretrial stage by permitting the accused and the defense access to investigative material only after the preliminary investigation was completed. By law defendants may confront witnesses, present evidence, and examine the government's case in advance of a trial, but defendants and their attorneys had very little ability to challenge government witnesses or police, while courts tended to accept prosecution materials routinely. In particular, the law prohibits police officers from testifying in their official capacities unless they were witnesses or victims in a case. Judges were reluctant to challenge police experts, hampering a defendant's ability to mount a credible defense. Judges' control over witness lists and over the determination of the relevance of potential witnesses in criminal cases also impeded the defense. Defense attorneys complained that judges at times did not allow them to request the attendance at trial of defense witnesses. According to lawyers and domestic and international human rights observers, including the Council of Europe's human rights commissioner, the prosecution retained a dominant position in the criminal justice system.

Human rights lawyers expressed concern regarding a December 2015 constitutional amendment that prohibits the use in court of evidence obtained in violation only of fundamental rights. Prior to the amendment, the constitution had a broader prohibition against the use of evidence obtained in violation of any law.

Defendants, prosecutors, and injured parties have the right of appeal and often exercised it.

There was an expectation that judges would find the accused guilty in almost every case, and the vast majority of criminal cases sent to trial, including many weak cases, resulted in conviction. According to court statistics, the acquittal rate during the first 10 months of the year was approximately 4 percent.

In a rare acquittal, on April 15, trial judge Narine Hovakimyan acquitted and released from detention Karen Kungurtsev, who had spent more than two and one-half years in prison after trial awaiting a verdict on charges of attempted murder. The victim's family supported Kungurtsev's claim of innocence, convinced that the real killer of Davit Hovakimyan was the son of a NSS official who had used his position to influence police and the prosecutors to pin the crime on Kungurtsev. The prosecution appealed the acquittal, and as of November 28, the appeal trial continued.

**Political Prisoners and Detainees**

According to human rights' NGOs and the political opposition, there were political prisoners and detainees in the country.

Human rights organizations considered Gevorg Safaryan, a member of the New Armenia political movement, a political detainee. On January 1, authorities arrested him, after a scuffle between police and a number of activists, including Safaryan, for attempting to put a festive tree in Yerevan's Freedom Square. Safaryan, who maintained he and others suffered from police brutality, was detained for violence towards police and faced a maximum sentence if convicted of five years' imprisonment. As of November 28, his trial continued, with witnesses presenting conflicting testimonies.

Human rights NGOs among others also considered as political detainees many of those who faced criminal charges in connection with the July 17-30 events, with the exception of the armed group members who occupied the police building. For example, on July 29 and 30, police detained three members of the Heritage Party (Armen Martisoryan, Hovsep Khurshudyan, and David Sanasaryan) and political activists Andrias Ghukasyan and Davit Hovhannisyan, allegedly for organizing mass disorders.  Authorities claimed that the political figures were instigating violence and leading the crowd to join the armed men in the occupied police building but reportedly could not corroborate the charge.  On August 17, 19, and 24, separate courts released Martirosyan, Sanasaryan and Khurshudyan on bail; Hovhannisyan and Ghukasyan remained in custody as of November 28.  On November 14, the prosecutor general's office announced that it would combine the criminal case on the organization of mass disorders on July 29, with the criminal case against the Sasna Tsrer group and file charges.

Volodia Avetisyan, a war veteran who, prior to his 2018 arrest, was actively engaged in veterans' protests for improved social protection, continued to serve a six-year sentence for a conviction of fraud at year's end.  He maintained his innocence and claimed authorities targeted him after he refused to accept bribes in exchange for stopping his civic activism.

**Civil Judicial Procedures and Remedies**

Although citizens had access to courts to file lawsuits seeking damages for human rights violations, the courts were widely perceived as corrupt.  Citizens also had access to the ombudsman's office as well as the possibility of challenging in the Constitutional Court the constitutionality of laws and legal acts that violated their fundamental rights and freedoms.  While the Constitutional Court exercised its power to determine the constitutionality of statutes in dozens of cases, lower courts, which are subordinate to the Court of Cassation rather than to the Constitutional Court, enforced its decisions unevenly.

Citizens who exhaust domestic legal remedies may appeal cases involving alleged government violations of the European Convention on Human Rights to the ECHR.  The government generally complied with ECHR awards of monetary compensation but did not meaningfully review the cases on which the ECHR had ruled.  When ruling on a case to which a prior ECHR decision applied, courts often did not follow the applicable ECHR precedent.

**f. Arbitrary or Unlawful Interference with Privacy, Family, Home, or Correspondence**

The constitution prohibits unauthorized searches and provides for the rights to privacy and confidentiality of communications.  Law enforcement organizations did not always abide by these prohibitions.

Authorities may not legally wiretap telephones, intercept correspondence, or conduct searches without obtaining the permission of a judge based on compelling evidence of criminal activity.  The constitution, however, stipulates exceptions when confidentiality of communication may be restricted without a court order when necessary to protect state security and conditioned by the special status of those in communication.  Although law enforcement bodies generally adhered to legal procedures, attorneys claimed judges often authorized wiretaps, the interception of correspondence, and searches without receiving the compelling evidence required by law, rendering the legal procedures largely a formality.  Authorities reportedly tapped the telephone communications, e-mail, and other digital communications of individuals the government wanted to keep under scrutiny, including human rights defenders, activists and political figures.

**Section 2. Respect for Civil Liberties, Including:**

**a. Freedom of Speech and Press**

The constitution and law provide for freedom of speech and press, but the government's respect for these rights was uneven.  Print, online, and broadcast media generally expressed views sympathetic to their owners or advertisers, a mix of government officials and oligarchs.  There were several instances of violence toward journalists in connection with their coverage of peaceful protests.

Freedom of Speech and Expression:  While most individuals were able to criticize the government publicly or privately and discuss matters of general public interest without fear of reprisal, members of media often exercised self-censorship to avoid official harassment.

On August 7, the independent media portal Medialab.am organized an open-air exhibit of its political cartoons following refusals from various hall owners in Yerevan to rent it exhibition space.  On the night of the show, Medialab director Marianna Grigoryan's car was burglarized, and all posters and T-shirts with the cartoons intended to be displayed during the weeklong show were stolen.  On September 30, police suspended the investigation after failing to identify the perpetrators.

Press and Media Freedoms:  Print and broadcast media generally lacked diversity of political opinion and objective reporting.  Private individuals or groups owned most newspapers, and newspapers, with limited circulation, tended to reflect the political leanings of proprietors and financial backers, who in turn were often close to the government.  Broadcast media, particularly national television, remained the primary source of news and information for the majority of the population. Politicians in the ruling party and politically connected executives owned most stations, and the stations presented one-sided views of events.  Regional television channels provided some alternative viewpoints, often through externally produced content.  On politically sensitive topics, however, media overwhelmingly provided only government-supported views and analysis.

The few independent media outlets, mostly online, were not self-sustainable and survived through international funding.  During the year one such outlet, *Armenia Now*, regarded by media experts and the public as providing professional and unbiased content, closed after donations from an American-Armenian philanthropist ended.  According to media experts, even a permanent readership was insufficient to save an outlet from financial collapse in an environment where financial patronage often controlled content.

In December 2015, the National Assembly changed the law regulating the issuance of channels on the digital broadcast network.  Media watchdogs criticized the amendments, asserting they sought to consolidate progovernment outlets' control over the media market.

The government did not generally control the content of online media, which together with social networks, served as an important alternative source of information.  Unlike broadcast media, online media and social networks tended to provide diverse political opinions.  The livestreaming of important political events gained in importance among the online media outlets, especially during public protests.  Nevertheless, online media also showed signs of the influence by politically connected owners and advertisers.  There were credible reports that both online and broadcast media outlets were in the hands of a few government-affiliated individuals.  Traditional and online media ownership remained nontransparent.

<u>Violence and Harassment</u>:  Police targeted journalists covering public protests and subjected them to violence.  As of August 9, authorities charged four police officers with violence against journalists.  Investigations continued at year's end.

On July 29, police and armed civilians acting in coordination with them used stun grenades, wooden clubs, and metal bars against journalists and damaged or seized their equipment while dispersing a rally of persons sympathetic with the demands of the Sasna Tsrer group.  As a result, 24 reporters and operators suffered injuries.

Before the rally's dispersal, police instructed the journalists to move away from the main crowd for safety.  According to numerous accounts, after journalists complied, police fired the first stun grenades toward them.

The Prosecutor General's Office and SIS initiated criminal investigations into the violence.  Police also announced that they were seeking to identify the civilians who beat the journalists.  While police searched for those involved, reporters and social media users posted photos of three such "civilians", identifying one as Arshak Hakobyan, the head of security for national Chief of Police Vladimir Gasparyan, and two others as Gasparyan's personal bodyguards.  According to official information eight civilians were charged in connection with this case, four of whom--Seyran Karapetyan, Vladmir Mkhitaryan, Davit Sargsyan, and Karen Grigoryan--were convicted and sentenced to one year in prison and fined 200,000 drams ($420).  Authorities forwarded the cases against three others, Gor Khachatryan, Garegin Hovsepyan, and Tigran Aharanoyan, to the courts, while the case against Sargis Sahakyan remained under investigation.  As of November 25, no law enforcement officers had been charged and the investigation continued at year's end (see sections 1.c., 1.d., and 2.b.).

On August 9, more than a year after police beat and detained journalists while dispersing a peaceful June 2015 protest in downtown Yerevan, SIS announced it had charged four police officers, Davit Perikhanyan, Kostan Budaghyan, Tachat Noratunkyan, and Artur Ayvazyan, with obstructing the activities of four reporters in this case.  Media NGOs considered the decision inadequate, in view of the fact that two dozen journalists had suffered from police abuse, which, they maintained, high-ranking police officials had ordered.  As of November 28, the trial against the four officers and the investigation into the other instances of abuse continued.

<u>Censorship and Content Restrictions</u>:  Media outlets, particularly broadcasters, feared reprisals for reports critical of the government.  Such reprisals could include lawsuits, the threat of losing a broadcast license, selective tax investigation, or loss of revenue when advertisers learned an outlet was in disfavor with the government.  Fear of retribution resulted in media self-censorship.  The escalation of the armed conflict with Azerbaijan in April was marked by a higher degree of self-censorship by media outlets as well as social media users, who uncritically presented only government or de facto Nagorno-Karabakh authorities' reports on the conflict.

**Internet Freedom**

Individuals and groups could generally engage in the expression of views via the internet, including by e-mail. Some human rights activists and opposition party members claimed, however, that authorities monitored their e-mail and other internet communications (see section 1.f.). On the morning of July 17, the first day of the armed takeover of the Erebuni police compound, access to Facebook was inexplicably unavailable for approximately 45 minutes. This was the only case of possible government disruption of internet access during the year.

The International Telecommunication Union estimated that 58 percent of the population used the internet in 2015.

**Academic Freedom and Cultural Events**

There were some reports of government restrictions on academic freedom and cultural events.

Both the administration and student councils of the most prominent state universities were politicized and affiliated with the RPA. For example, the president of the Board of Trustees of Yerevan State University, Serzh Sargsyan, was president of the country. Government ministers led, or were members of, the boards of trustees of other universities. According to human rights observers, student councils in most universities experienced various forms of pressure to support the interests of the university rather than those of the student body and to keep the student body focused on nonpolitical and less sensitive issues.

During elections as well as the December 2015 referendum, authorities used public educational institutions (schools, universities, and even kindergartens) to support RPA activities to influence the youth. Lack of employment opportunities for teachers and scholars limited their willingness to refuse to engage in such political activity. During the December 2015 constitutional referendum, there were numerous reports of school principals pressing employees to promote the "yes" campaign for constitutional changes pushed by the ruling party. Many school administrators also participated in referendum commissions, creating a potential for election violations. Media reported on one teacher, Karpis Pashoyan, who lost his job for refusing to promote the "yes" campaign and trying to prevent referendum fraud.

**b. Freedom of Peaceful Assembly and Association**

**Freedom of Assembly**

The constitution and the law provide for freedom of assembly.  While many small-scale gatherings occurred without interference during the year, in multiple instances the government used violence and excessive force against demonstrators or detained them arbitrarily and otherwise hampered peaceful gatherings.

From July 17 to July 30 and subsequently, while the Sasna Tsrer group held hostage the Patrol-Guard Service Regiment of the Erebuni Police in Yerevan, persons sympathetic to the group or their political demands held numerous demonstrations.  Protesters mainly gathered on Freedom Square or on Khorenatsi Street and staged marches in the streets of Yerevan.  Police interfered with the marches, used force, and arbitrarily detained hundreds of individuals participating in the protests, subjecting many to violence, often asserting that the gatherings lacked a permit.  In its report on the events between July 17 and August 5, the Helsinki Committee of Armenia stated the rallies "were accompanied by brutal interventions and unprecedented violations committed by police."

The Brussels-based NGO International Partnership for Human Rights (IPHR) within the framework of Civic Solidarity Platform (CSP), an international coalition of human rights NGOs, conducted a fact-finding mission to the country from July 28 to August 1 and described the demonstrations as largely peaceful.  CSP monitors also observed the efforts by demonstration leaders to restrain the public from acts of violence.  The CSP looked into two instances in which police used nonlethal weapons against demonstrators on July 20 and July 29, concluding that such weapons were justified on July 20, when the crowd acted aggressively.  The CSP concluded that police used excessive force subsequently, after the demonstrators had dispersed.  According to the CSP, police use of rocket-projected or hand-held stun grenades on July 29 was disproportionate, excessive, and indiscriminate and employed without advance warning.

According to legal experts, the police practice of arbitrarily detaining peaceful demonstrators constituted a de facto application of "administrative detention" that was outlawed in 2005.  According to the legal experts and IPHR, police employed detention primarily as a means of stopping what were largely peaceful protests.

The Helsinki Committee, in a report covering the observation of 126 assemblies between July 2015 and June, noted that police presence at those rallies was disproportionate to the number of participants and that police used blanket restrictions to ban rallies in certain venues, such as in front of the president's office.  The report cited significant police interference in 29 cases, including arrests, violence, and forcible removal of participants from one venue to another. The report also questioned the arbitrary interpretation by police of freedom of assembly laws as well as police methods, such as giving orders or instructions to participants without an accompanying justification or reason and then charging them with resisting a "lawful demand" when they did not comply.

According to official sources, as of November 25, SIS had not charged anyone or identified any suspects in connection with the charges of abuse of official authority related to the alleged abuses by law enforcement officers during the July protests.

**Freedom of Association**

The constitution and law provide this right, and the government generally respected it. The government did not provide a legal framework to support the financial sustainability of NGOs. The law does not permit such organizations to charge fees for their services, create endowments, or engage directly in profit-generating activities to fund their operations and achieve their statutory goals. As a result NGOs were dependent on grants and donations.

**c. Freedom of Religion**

See the Department of State's *International Religious Freedom Report* at www.state.gov/religiousfreedomreport/.

**d. Freedom of Movement, Internally Displaced Persons, Protection of Refugees, and Stateless Persons**

The law provides for freedom of internal movement, foreign travel, emigration, and repatriation, and the government generally respected these rights.

<u>Abuse of Migrants, Refugees, and Stateless Persons</u>:  Authorities did not generally release asylum seekers serving sentences for illegal entry into the country after registering their asylum applications. Instead, they required them to remain in pretrial detention pending the outcome of their asylum application or to serve the remainder of their sentences, despite a provision in the criminal code exempting asylum seekers from criminal liability. The Office of the UN High Commissioner for Refugees (UNHCR) reported that authorities detained two Afghan asylum seekers for illegal border crossing on October 2015. The detention took place despite their application for asylum almost immediately after their apprehension at the border and despite the fact that a final decision on their asylum claims was

pending as of November 28.  Due to their prolonged detention, both individuals developed severe physical and psychological health problems.  On November 15, a trial court convicted both asylum seekers for illegally crossing the border and sentenced them to three years' imprisonment, the minimum sentence for this offense.

According to UNHCR, while the overall quality of procedures and decision making for determination of refugee status improved, concerns remained regarding adjudication of cases of asylum seekers of certain religious profiles.  UNHCR observed that security considerations permeated all aspects of the asylum procedure and implementation of refugee policies.  UNHCR noted with concern the increasing influence of NSS on asylum decision making by the State Migration Service and cases of prolonged detention of non-Christian asylum seekers who had entered the country illegally.  For example, starting at the end of 2015, authorities applied stricter approaches to asylum seekers from Iraq who were not ethnically Armenian.

According to UNHCR, questions remained as to the circumstances of the departure of one asylum seeker from Bahrain who had been detained in the country in connection with an Interpol Red Notice.  Human rights NGOs reported that authorities had forced the asylum seeker to agree to depart for a third country as an alternative to extradition.

Authorities cooperated with UNHCR and other humanitarian organizations in providing protection and assistance to internally displaced persons (IDPs), refugees, returning refugees, asylum seekers, stateless persons, or other persons of concern.

Foreign Travel:  Citizens must obtain exit visas to leave the country on either a temporary or a permanent basis.  Citizens could routinely purchase exit visas for temporary travel outside the country within one day of application for approximately 1,000 drams ($2.10) for each year of validity.

**Internally Displaced Persons**

As of May 2015, according to the Internal Displacement Monitoring Center, approximately 8,400 IDPs of the roughly 65,000 households evacuated during 1988-94 were still living in displacement.  Some of the country's IDPs and former refugees lacked adequate housing and had limited economic opportunities.

**Protection of Refugees**

Access to Asylum:  The law provides for granting asylum or refugee status, and the government has established a system for providing protection to refugees.  The law takes into account of specific needs of children, persons with mental disabilities and trauma survivors.  The amended law also allows detention centers to receive asylum applications.

The increase in violence along the Line of Contact and Armenia-Azerbaijan international border April 1-5 led to displacement of civilians from villages close to the Line of Contact.  Some of the displaced remained in Nagorno-Karabakh, while others entered Armenia to seek refuge.  According to UNHCR observers, the overwhelming majority of displaced persons consisted of women, children, and elderly persons, primarily from the villages close to the Line of Contact.  UNHCR estimated the total numbers of displaced at approximately 2,300 at the peak of displacement, with approximately 540 remaining in the country as of November 8.

Access to Basic Services:  Authorities continued to offer ethnic Armenians from Syria who remained in the country a choice of various protection options, namely expedited naturalization, a residence permit, or refugee status.  Quick access to citizenship gave persons displaced from Syria the same legal rights to health care and most other social services as other citizens.  Housing allocated to refugees was often in limited supply and in poor condition and remained the biggest concern for them, as well as employment.  Many displaced families relied on a rental subsidy program supported by UNHCR and diaspora organizations.  In 2015 authorities opened an integration house with places for 29 refugees and offered refugees accommodation free of charge during the first months after they acquired refugee status.  Language differences with Syrian-Armenian refugees who spoke a different dialect created barriers to employment and, initially, education.  In addition refugees faced many of the same social and economic hardships that confronted the general population.  Refugees who were not ethnic Armenians needed three years of legal residence in the country to be naturalized.

Durable Solutions:  Authorities offered ethnic Armenians from Syria who remained in the country the option of expedited naturalization.  On July 21, the government adopted a concept document outlining its goals concerning the integration of persons granted asylum and refugee status as well as of long-term migrants.  According to UNHCR, while in principle a welcome step to enhance the legal framework for the protection of refugees, the concept did not cover Syrians who had obtained Armenian citizenship, thus excluding from coverage the majority of displaced Syrians who had arrived in country since the beginning of the conflict.  The concept also does not address critical aspects of integration, such as language needs and access to education.

**Stateless Persons**

As of June 30, according to the police passport and visas department, there were approximately 300 stateless persons in the country.  In addition authorities considered approximately 1,400 refugees from Azerbaijan to be stateless.  In May amendments to citizenship legislation contributed to the prevention and reduction of statelessness.  The amendments provided Armenian nationality to stateless children born on the country's territory, including children born of foreigners who held Armenian citizenship but did not meet the requirement for transmission to their children.  These changes de facto affected those born on the territory of Nagorno-Karabakh, who had access to Armenian identity documents when requested.  There was anecdotal evidence that some persons without documents were stateless or at risk of being stateless because they had entered the country irregularly or lived in remote areas and still held Soviet documents.  Rejected applicants for naturalization did not have the right to appeal.  There was no clear procedure for the determination of statelessness and no national legislation on the rights of stateless persons.

**Section 3. Freedom to Participate in the Political Process**

Although the constitution and laws provide citizens the ability to choose their government in free and fair periodic elections based on universal and equal suffrage and conducted by secret ballot, the government continued to interfere throughout the electoral process via practices designed to ensure the dominance of the ruling RPA.

In December 2015 the country held a constitutional referendum, which, in conjunction with subsequent amendments to the electoral code, resulted in shifting the state structure from a semipresidential to a parliamentary republic, eliminating direct election of the president and mayors of two major cities and introducing a complex proportional electoral system that many characterized as semimajoritarian.

**Elections and Political Participation**

<u>Recent Elections</u>: The country held a presidential election in 2013 and National Assembly elections in 2012. The OSCE's Office for Democratic Institutions and Human Rights (ODIHR) described the presidential election as well administered but with shortcomings, including an uneven playing field, serious election-day violations, and concerns about the integrity of the electoral process. Reports of bribery of voters, large-scale administrative abuses favoring incumbents, evidence of impostors voting in place of absentee voters, and the presence of unauthorized organized groups at many precincts undermined the process and further discredited the institution of elections in the public eye. Similar flaws marred the 2012 National Assembly elections, in which OSCE/ ODIHR found credible allegations of vote buying, deficiencies in the complaints and appeals process, and shortcomings in the electoral code despite improvements.

In December 2015 citizens voted in a referendum, initiated by the president, to amend the constitution and move from a semipresidential to a parliamentary system of government. Many civil society organizations and some opposition political forces contended the constitutional changes did not respond to any demand in society and represented an effort by the ruling party to prolong the power of the country's existing leadership. The conduct of the constitutional referendum was peaceful, but there were credible media reports indicating systemic fraud by those affiliated with the government. There were also reports that officials threatened and pressured employees in the large state-run sector to vote for the referendum.

Domestic observers and media noted such irregularities during the referendum as ballot box stuffing, vote buying, multiple voting by the same individuals, and fraudulent vote tabulation. The government initiated numerous investigations related to referendum fraud and violations, none of which resulted in a prison sentence. In the 42 cases tried, 36 persons were sentenced to fines and 10 received a suspended sentence, with one other person acquitted at the appeals court level.

<u>Political Parties and Political Participation</u>: While the law does not overly restrict the registration or activity of political parties, authorities suppressed political pluralism in other ways.

Continuing complaints that the government used its administrative and legal resources to discourage financial contributions to opposition parties, including by selective tax investigations, served to limit their activities. Civil society organizations reported incumbents abused government resources during election campaigns, including by threatening to deprive families of social benefits and students of scholarships as punishment for refusing to vote for the incumbent or support the constitutional reform.

Affiliation with the ruling party reportedly helped individuals maintain and further their careers in both the public and private sectors.  Numerous reports from local observers indicated some community leaders who ran as independents either joined the RPA or became RPA loyalists after they were elected, due to concern they could not function effectively otherwise.  Local communities depended in part on state funding, and reports suggested the level of support community leaders received from the state budget often depended on their party affiliation.  Similarly, within public schools, universities, state medical facilities, and other publically funded institutions, there were allegations that individuals had to be RPA members or loyalists to attain leadership positions and resources.  According to media and other reports, becoming a ruling party member or loyalist paved the way for better grades, scholarships, and other types of favorable treatment.  The ruling party and its candidates allegedly abused administrative resources at public and some private enterprises to intimidate employers and to ensure their support.

Media reports, human rights NGOs, and some opposition political party leaders alleged that authorities created, managed, and coopted opposition parties and politicians.  The allegations--whether justified or not--were yet another factor diminishing public trust in the overall political process.

There were complaints that well-connected business owners funneled a portion of their profits to the ruling party or to parties affiliated with the ruling political elite in return for economic advantage in the form of limited or no taxation.  There were also allegations that the government discriminated against members of opposition political parties in hiring decisions.

<u>Participation of Women and Minorities</u>:  The hierarchical and patriarchal nature of society inhibited participation by women in political life and in decision-making positions in the public sector.  At year's end there were 13 women in the 131-seat National Assembly, three in the cabinet of 18 ministers, and no female governors in the country's 10 regions.  Only 10 of the 65 elected Yerevan City Council members were women.

**Section 4. Corruption and Lack of Transparency in Government**

The law provides criminal penalties for conviction of corruption by officials, but the government did not implement the law effectively, and officials often engaged in corrupt practices with impunity.  There were numerous allegations of government corruption.  According to the World Economic Forum's *Global Competitiveness Report* for 2015-16, corruption represented one of the most problematic obstacles to doing business in the country.  Freedom House's *Nations in Transit 2016* report noted that the government efforts to combat widespread corruption remained superficial.

Corruption:  Although the constitution prohibits individuals engaged in entrepreneurial activity from holding public office, company executives and oligarchs occupied seats in the National Assembly, and various government officials used their offices to promote their private business interests.  In the view of many observers, oligarchs linked to the government or holding government posts monopolized the economy.  Moreover, authorities reportedly ignored media and other reports implicating government officials in corrupt practices.

There were numerous media reports of systemic government corruption in areas ranging from construction, public administration, the judiciary, procurement practices, the provision of grants by the state (including the presidential administration), health care, taxation, law enforcement, education, and the military.  There were also allegations of embezzlement of state funds, the involvement of government officials in questionable business activities, and tax and customs privileges for government-linked companies.

Following the April escalation of the Nagorno-Karabakh conflict, allegations of poor conditions of the army due to mismanagement and misallocation of funds and other corrupt practices within the Ministry of Defense led authorities to announce anticorruption measures, including investigations and the dismissal of senior defense officials involved in procurement.  Despite high-level commitments to take concrete measures and to reduce unnecessary government spending, the only visible result was the reduction of the government's vehicle fleet.

On April 4, the investigative online publication *Hetq*, carried an expose of the offshore assets of Mihran Poghosyan, head of the Judicial Acts Compulsory Enforcement Service (CES) under the Ministry of Justice.  According to the report, Poghosyan used his official position as well as the resources of the CES to advance his various business interests.  For example, one of Poghosyan's Panama-based companies appraised properties for auction by the CES.  On April 18, Poghosyan resigned, stating he did not want his name to be associated with others exposed in the report.  On April 29, the SIS announced that it had initiated a criminal investigation into the facts presented by *Hetq*, on charges of illegal entrepreneurship, which is punishable by up to two years' imprisonment. As of November 25, the investigation continued although no charges had been brought against Poghosyan or anyone else in this case.

Financial Disclosure: The law requires high-ranking public officials and their families to file annual asset declarations; these were partially available to the public on the internet. There were administrative penalties for noncompliance or for filing false declarations, but the Ethics Commission for High-ranking Officials, responsible for collecting and monitoring the declarations, lacked authority to verify their accuracy or origins of the declared income or to penalize officials for false declarations. Many public officials, including judges, and National Assembly members and their spouses, disclosed large sums of unexplained income and assets, including large personal gifts and proceeds from providing loans. Authorities failed to investigate discrepancies or unexplained wealth identified in these declarations.

Public Access to Information: While the law provides for public access to government information, some government bodies and officials were reluctant to grant it. According to the NGO Freedom of Information Center of Armenia (FOICA) and the Transparency International Anticorruption Center, the biggest challenge remained governmental bodies that created the impression of satisfying freedom of information requests but provided answers that were either irrelevant or incomplete. As a result NGOs initiated more freedom of information cases in courts. According to FOICA, most freedom of information suits filed in recent years resulted in courts calling on the government to release more accurate information, but the courts usually balked at penalizing officials who failed to comply.

**Section 5. Governmental Attitude Regarding International and Nongovernmental Investigation of Alleged Violations of Human Rights**

A number of domestic and international human rights groups generally operated without government restrictions, investigating and publishing their findings on human rights cases. Although government officials were at times cooperative and responsive to their views, some also occasionally harassed activists.

Authorities generally agreed to requests for meetings from domestic NGO monitors and followed some of their recommendations, particularly those related to social welfare, education and local matters. The government also consulted with NGOs on anticorruption matters; these did not result in follow up actions, however.  The government failed to take significant action in response to NGO allegations of mistreatment and abuse by law enforcement bodies.  In instances when officials initiated investigations, they typically maintained they could not corroborate the allegations.

Authorities harassed civic activists and citizens who engaged in peaceful protests.  On July 26-27, police detained Levon Barseghyan, the head of a Gyumri-based anticorruption watchdog, the Asparez Journalists Club, detaining him for more 16 hours without access to a lawyer, his family, or basic necessities, allegedly for possession of a small folding knife.  Investigators released him on July 29 after determining the knife was not an illegal weapon.  Barseghyan and his lawyer claimed the detention was illegal and connected to Barseghyan's public activism.

During the year human rights organizations and the media reported on the continued harassment of and threats against human rights defender Marina Poghosyan.  Poghosyan's NGO, Veles, provided legal support to victims of moneylenders allegedly linked to the government.

On October 21, members of the Armenian organization International Humanitarian Development made allegations on the Russian website, Sputnik Armenia against prominent Armenian organizations, presenting them as threats to national security and plotting revolutions in the country.

<u>Government Human Rights Bodies</u>:  The Office of the Human Rights Defender (the ombudsman) has a mandate to protect human rights and fundamental freedoms from abuse at all levels of government.  On January 12, the country's third ombudsman, Karen Andreasyan, unexpectedly resigned without explanation, amid media speculation regarding growing political pressure on him from the ruling RPA and the executive branch.  On February 23, the National Assembly affirmed Arman Tatoyan to replace Karen Andreasyan.  The office served as an effective advocate, publishing issue-specific and routine reports on human rights problems.  In particular, it addressed and brought to the government's attention human rights violations, illegal detentions, and missteps during the forceful dispersal of protesters by police in July.

**Section 6. Discrimination, Societal Abuses, and Trafficking in Persons**

**Women**

<u>Rape and Domestic Violence</u>:  Rape is a criminal offense, and conviction carries a maximum sentence of 15 years; in the absence of a specific domestic violence law, general rape statutes applied to the prosecution of spousal rape.  Domestic violence was similarly prosecuted under general statutes dealing with violence.

Spousal abuse and violence against women appeared widespread.  According to the Asian Development Bank's July 2015 *Armenia Gender Assessment*, gender-based violence, especially domestic violence, was one of the most critical problems faced by women in the country.  Surveys by the government and women's organizations confirmed the assessment that domestic violence was widespread, affecting between 25 to 66 percent of women (depending how broad the definition of domestic violence).  Authorities did not effectively prosecute domestic violence.

Rape, spousal abuse, and domestic violence was underreported due to social stigma, the absence of female police officers and investigators, and at times police reluctance to act.  According to local observers, most domestic violence was not reported because survivors were afraid of physical harm, apprehensive that police would return them to their husbands, or ashamed to disclose their family problems.  There were also reports that police, especially outside of Yerevan, were reluctant to act in such cases and discouraged women from filing complaints.  A majority of domestic violence cases were considered under the law as offenses of low or medium seriousness.  In such instances a survivor might decline to press charges or perpetrators pressured them to withdraw charges or recant previous testimony.

Two local NGOs, the Women's Support Center and the Women's Rights Center, maintained domestic violence hotlines and three shelters and provided various services to the victim.  The shelters were insufficient to meet the needs of all victims in the country.  While international funding sustained the shelters, there were few realistic alternatives for sustainable, local funding.

Between 2010 and 2015, the Coalition to Stop Violence against Women recorded the killing of 30 women by an existing or former partner or a family member.  According to a coalition study published in May, many of these women had sought help from family or state institutions before being killed.  Local organizations maintained that police inaction and lenient sentences for partners convicted of abuse contributed to such deaths.  During the year there were several instances in which courts reportedly issued minimal fines to husbands who had abused their wives for years.

On July 8, Vladik Martirosyan attacked his former wife, Taguhi Mansuryan, and her parents with an axe. Mansuryan's mother died immediately, while Mansuryan and her father were hospitalized in serious condition. Martirosyan was previously convicted of domestic abuse but received a six-month suspended sentence.

Sexual Harassment: Although the law addresses lewd acts and indecent behavior, it does not specifically prohibit sexual harassment. While recent public data on the extent of the problem was unavailable, observers believed sexual harassment of women in the workplace was widespread. According to the Asian Development Bank's *Armenia Gender Assessment*, sexual harassment in the workplace was a factor limiting women's job choices and opportunities for advancement.

Reproductive Rights: The law gives couples and individuals the right to decide the number, spacing, and timing of their children; manage their reproductive health; and have the information and means necessary to do so, free from discrimination, coercion, or violence. The husband and his parents often made decisions the spacing and timing of a couple's children. Skilled attendance during childbirth was more accessible in large towns and other population centers where birthing facilities were located. There were reports that women, especially in rural or remote areas, had insufficient access to general and reproductive health care services. In its 2014 report, the UN Committee on Economic, Social, and Cultural Rights (CESCR) expressed concern regarding the limited availability of contraception.

Discrimination: Men and women enjoy equal legal status in the judicial system, but discrimination based on gender was a continuing problem in both the public and private sectors. There were reports of discrimination against women with respect to occupation and employment (see section 7.d.). Women remained underrepresented in leadership positions in all branches and at all levels of government (see section 3).

CESCR's report expressed concern regarding deeply rooted patriarchal attitudes and stereotypes regarding the role of women and men in the family and in society. According to gender experts, the education system at all levels reinforced these attitudes. A 2015 World Bank study examined teaching materials and textbooks of high school classes and found the books gave strong preference to men in all forms of representation, including texts and illustrations, while women were less visible or portrayed in stereotypical way.

<u>Gender-biased Sex Selection</u>:  According to the National Statistical Service, the boy to girl sex-at-birth ratio decreased from 114 to 100 in 2014 and from 112 to 100 for the first half of the year.  In May 2015 the Ministry of Health and the Ministry of Labor and Social Affairs approved a mid-term program to prevent sex selective abortions, establishing a working group to coordinate governmental efforts in this regard.  According to the UN Population Fund, joint programs by the government and international and local NGOs to increase awareness of this problem accounted for the slightly positive improvement in the first half of the year.

**Children**

<u>Birth Registration</u>:  Children derive citizenship from one or both parents.  Birth registration is the responsibility of parents, who must present the birth certificate to the hospital before checking out.  Absence of a birth certificate could result in denial of public services.

<u>Education</u>:  Although education is free and compulsory through grade nine, in practice it was not universal.  According to the UN Children's Fund (UNICEF), children with disabilities and from socially vulnerable families faced systematic disadvantages in their access to schools and to the use of educational services (see Persons with Disabilities, below).  Children from disadvantaged families and communities lacked access to early learning programs, despite government efforts to raise preschool enrollment.  Enrollment and attendance rates for children from ethnic minority groups, in particular Yezidis, Kurds, and Molokans, were significantly lower than average, and dropout rates after the eighth grade were higher.  UNICEF expressed concern about the integration into the local community of an increasing number of refugee children from Syria, Iraq, and Ukraine.  Poor school infrastructure, particularly for preschools, including inadequate heating, water, and sanitation, remained a problem, with vast majority of school buildings not complying with basic safety standards.

<u>Child Abuse</u>:  Although comprehensive statistics on violence against children were unavailable, such violence appeared to be a problem, especially for those living in institutions and in socially vulnerable families.  Irregular exchanges of fire between Armenian and Azerbaijani forces put children living in border areas at risk of injury or death.  According to UNICEF, the lack of official, unified data on violence against children limited the government's ability to design adequate national responses and preventive measures.  There were no official referral procedures for children who became victims of violence, including sexual

violence, and referrals were not mandatory for professionals working with children, excluding doctors.

The Women's Resource Center noted an increase in sexual assault against minors and that the victims assisted were younger than in the previous years. The center also reported instances in which young victims were stigmatized, mocked in their communities, and expelled from school.

Early and Forced Marriage:  According to UNICEF, 7 percent of children (both boys and girls) married by age 18, the legal minimum age.  Early marriage of girls was reportedly more frequent within the Yezidi communities, but the government took no measures to document the scale or address the practice.

Sexual Exploitation of Children:  Antitrafficking statutes prohibit the sexual exploitation of children and carry sentences of seven to 15 years in prison, depending on whether aggravating circumstances are present.  Child pornography is punishable by imprisonment for up to seven years.  The minimum age for consensual sex is 16.

Institutionalized Children:  The government maintained 36 residential facilities housing approximately 3,800 children, the majority of whom had at least one living parent.  Experts believed corruption and poverty were the primary impediments to deinstitutionalization, since the government based its funding for institutions on the number of residents, and many families were unable to financially support their children's needs.  On average the government spent more than 5.46 billion drams ($13 million) annually to maintain such institutions. According to UNICEF and other observers, institutionalized children were at risk of physical and psychological violence by peers and by staff.  UNICEF notified state officials regarding numerous violations of food and health standards, but authorities made few improvements.  The government worked with UNICEF and NGOs, using foreign funds, to reduce the number of children in institutions and to establish community and family-based alternatives as well as inclusive schools for children with special needs.

International Child Abductions:  The country is a party to the 1980 Hague Convention on the Civil Aspects of International Child Abduction.  See the Department of State's *Annual Report on International Parental Child Abduction* at travel.state.gov/content/childabduction/en/legal/compliance.html.

**Anti-Semitism**

Observers estimated the country's Jewish population to be between 500 and 1,000 persons.  There were no reports of anti-Semitic acts.

**Trafficking in Persons**

See the Department of State's *Trafficking in Persons Report* at www.state.gov/j/tip/rls/tiprpt/.

**Persons with Disabilities**

The law prohibits discrimination against persons with any disability in employment, education, and access to health care and other state services, but discrimination remained a problem.  The law and a special government decree require both new buildings and those under renovation, including schools, to be accessible to persons with disabilities.  Very few buildings or other facilities were accessible, even if newly constructed or renovated.  Many public buildings including schools and kindergartens were inaccessible which also deterred persons with disabilities from voting, since these buildings often served as polling stations during elections.  The Ministry of Labor and Social Affairs is responsible for protecting the rights of persons with disabilities but failed to carry out this mandate effectively.

According to a 2012 UNICEF survey, one in five children with disabilities did not attend school.  This was due to both discrimination and the lack of facilities to accommodate their needs.  In 2014 CESCR reported that, in spite of state efforts to expand the network of inclusive schools, officials did not fully implement the policy.  The law requires all public schools to become inclusive by 2025.

Persons with all types of disabilities experienced discrimination in every sphere, including access to health care, social and psychological rehabilitation, education, transportation, communication, employment, social protection, cultural events, and use of the internet.  Lack of access to information and communications was a particularly significant problem for persons with sensory disabilities.

Women with disabilities faced further discrimination, including in social acceptance and access to health and reproductive care, employment, and education, due to their gender.

Hospitals, residential care, and other facilities for persons with more significant disabilities remained substandard.

According to official data, more than 90 percent of persons with disabilities who were able to work were unemployed. In July 2015 the government introduced mandatory quotas for the employment of persons with disabilities for both public and private firms employing more than 100 persons.

Media reports alleged corruption and arbitrary rulings on the part of the Medical-social Expertise Commission, a governmental body under the Ministry of Labor and Social Affairs that determines a person's disability status. Disability status, in turn, determines eligibility for various social benefits.

**Acts of Violence, Discrimination, and Other Abuses Based on Sexual Orientation and Gender Identity**

Antidiscrimination laws do not apply to sexual orientation or gender identity. There were no hate crime laws or other criminal judicial mechanisms to aid in the prosecution of crimes against members of the LGBTI community. Societal attitudes toward LGBTI persons remained highly negative, with society generally viewing homosexuality as a medical affliction. Societal discrimination based on sexual orientation and gender identity negatively affected all aspects of life, including employment, housing, family relations, and access to education and health care. Transgender persons were especially vulnerable to physical and psychological abuse and harassment.

According to an assessment during the year by the NGO New Generation, transgender individuals desiring to undergo sex change procedures faced obstacles that included negative attitudes, lack of information, and absence of legal regulations. This led to numerous medical and other problems tied to the administration of hormones without medical supervision, underground surgeries, and problems obtaining passports and documenting a change in gender identity.

In May the NGO Public Information and Need of Knowledge (PINK Armenia) published its annual review of the human rights situation of LGBTI persons for 2015. According to the review, leading political party representatives and media affiliated with authorities employed "hate speech" toward members of the LGBTI community. Antigay rhetoric intensified during public discussions prior to the December 2015 referendum on constitutional amendments to ban same-sex marriages. According to the review, LGBTI persons experienced physical violence and threats of violence, blackmail, and harassment. Police were unresponsive to reports of such abuses and at times themselves mistreated LGBTI individuals, following and harassing them. According to the review, authorities did not prosecute a single hate crime complaint filed with police in 2015. LGBTI persons were also reluctant to report violations to relevant bodies due to fears of exposure and additional discriminatory treatment because of their complaint.

According to media reports, during a November 6 parliamentary discussion, three members of parliament (MP) from the ruling RPA, including the deputy speaker of the parliament, engaged in anti-LGBTI rhetoric, with one MP making a joke encouraging physical violence against LGBTI individuals.

According to PINK Armenia, in May a Karin folk dance group instructor, Harut Baghdasaryan, expelled Armenian-American dancer Kyle Khanidkyan after finding out that he was gay. According to media reports, the instructor told Khanidkyan that he did not belong to the "nation," that he was "not Armenian," and had no right to dance Armenian dances because he was gay.

Elements of media disseminated anti-LGBTI propaganda. LGBTI activists as well as human rights defenders working in the field received threats via social media and to be targets of hate speech.

Openly gay men were exempt from military service, purportedly because of concern that fellow soldiers would abuse them. An exemption, however, required a medical finding based on a psychological examination indicating an individual had a mental disorder; this information appeared in the individual's personal identification documents and was an obstacle to employment and to obtaining a driver's license. Gay men who served in the army reportedly faced physical and psychological abuse as well as blackmail.

**HIV and AIDS Social Stigma**

In the most recent demographic and health survey (conducted in 2010), approximately 86 percent of women and 84 percent of men reported having discriminatory attitudes towards persons with HIV/AIDS.

According to human rights groups, persons regarded as vulnerable to HIV/AIDS, such as sex workers (including transgender sex workers) and drug users, faced discrimination and violence from society as well as mistreatment by police.

The NGO Real World Real Life registered cases of men infected with HIV/AIDS during migrant work abroad who hid their condition from their wives. Having infected their wives, these men reportedly forbade them from seeking help and medication, although the men themselves underwent treatment. The NGO maintained that this was a manifestation of both domestic abuse and the social stigma associated with HIV/AIDS. A January 24 story on the Medialab.am website discussed the plight of an HIV/AIDS-infected pregnant woman who experienced significant discrimination from medical personnel throughout her pregnancy, including segregation from other patients and the unwillingness of medical personnel to provide her medical assistance while she was giving birth.

## Section 7. Worker Rights

### a. Freedom of Association and the Right to Collective Bargaining

The law protects the right of all workers to form and to join independent unions, except for personnel of the armed forces and law enforcement agencies. The law also provides for the right to strike, with the same exceptions, and permits collective bargaining. The law mandates a seven-day notification and mandatory mediation before a strike. The law stipulates that worker rights may not be restricted because of membership in a union. The list of justifiable grounds for firing a worker, enumerated in the labor code, does not include union activity.

The Ministry of Health State Health Inspectorate is responsible for conducting labor protection and safety inspections and the State Employment Agency of the Ministry of Labor and Social Affairs gets notification in case of mass layoffs to consider the possible employment options for newly unemployed. The government did not always effectively enforce labor rights. Resources, inspections, and remediation were inadequate. There were no specific penalties for violation of the right to freedom of association and collective bargaining; administrative and judicial procedures were subject to lengthy delays and appeals.

Labor organizations remained weak because of employer resistance, high unemployment, and poor economic conditions. Labor unions were generally inactive with the exception of those connected with the mining and chemical industries. According to domestic observers, the informal consent of the employer was required to establish a formal trade union.

### b. Prohibition of Forced or Compulsory Labor

The law prohibits all forms of forced and compulsory labor, and the government effectively enforced the law.  Resources, inspections, and remediation were adequate.  Penalties for violations ranged from five to 15 years in prison and were sufficiently stringent to deter violations.  During the first 10 months of the year, the Investigative Committee launched four investigations on suspicion of labor trafficking.

Also see the Department of State's *Trafficking in Persons Report* at www.state.gov/j/tip/rls/tiprpt/.

**c. Prohibition of Child Labor and Minimum Age for Employment**

There are laws and policies designed to protect children from exploitation in the workplace.  In most cases the minimum age for employment is 16, but children may work from age 14 with permission of a parent or a guardian.  The law allows children under age 14 to participate in the entertainment sector.  The maximum duration of the workweek is 24 hours for children who are 14 to 16 and 36 hours for children who are 16 to 18.  Persons under age 18 may not work overtime, in harmful, strenuous, or dangerous conditions, at night, or on holidays.  The authorities did not effectively enforce applicable law.  Penalties were insufficient to enforce compliance.

According to the *Armenian National Child Labor Survey 2015 Analytical Report* conducted by the National Statistical Service and the International Labor Organization, 11.6 percent of children between ages five and 17 were employed.  Most of the working children were involved in the agriculture, forestry and fishing sectors, while others worked in the sectors of trade, repair, transport, storage, accommodation, and food services.  Children were also involved in the trade of motor fuel, construction materials, medication, vehicle maintenance and repair works.  According to the survey, 39,300 children were employed, of whom 31,200 children were engaged in hazardous work, including work in hazardous industries (400 children), in designated hazardous occupations (600 children), long hours of work (1,200 children), work that involved carrying heavy loads and distances (17,200 children) and other forms of hazardous work (23,600 children).

Also see the Department of Labor's *Findings on the Worst Forms of Child Labor* at www.dol.gov/ilab/reports/child-labor/findings/.

**d. Discrimination with Respect to Employment and Occupation**

The amended constitution prohibits discrimination based on sex, race, skin color, ethnic or social origin, genetic features, language, religion, political opinion, belonging to a national minority, property status, birth, disability, age, or other personal or social circumstances.  Other laws and regulations specifically prohibit discrimination in employment and occupation based on gender.  The government did not effectively enforce the law.  There were no effective legal mechanisms to implement these regulations, and discrimination in employment and occupation occurred based on gender, age, presence of a disability, sexual orientation, HIV/AIDS status, and religion.  Administrative penalties were not sufficient to deter violations.

Women generally did not enjoy the same professional opportunities or wages as men, and employers often relegated them to more menial or low-paying jobs.  While providing for the "legal equality" of all parties in a workplace relationship, the labor code does not explicitly require equal pay for equal work.  According to World Bank data released during the year, more than one-half of women with intermediary education and one-third of women with advanced education did not participate in paid work.  According to the 2015 Asian Development Bank's *Armenia:  Country Gender Assessment*, a many women were engaged in informal work, leaving them without the protection of labor legislation.  Women also represented a larger share of the registered unemployed and it took them a longer time to find work.  According to a gender gap study of the UN Population Fund, *Diagnostic Study of Discrimination against Women*, released in March, the gap between average salaries of men and women in all economic spheres was almost 36 percent.

Many employers reportedly practiced age discrimination, most commonly requiring job applicants to be between ages 18 and 30.  Such discrimination appeared to be widespread, and authorities did not take any action to mitigate it.  Vacancy announcements specifying young and attractive women for various jobs were common.  Unemployed workers, particularly women, who were older than 40 had little chance of finding jobs appropriate to their education or skills.  LGBTI persons, as well as persons with disabilities also faced discrimination in employment.  Religious minorities faced discrimination in public employment.

### e. Acceptable Conditions of Work

The monthly minimum wage was 55,000 drams ($115).  According to the most recent official estimate, in 2015 the extreme poverty line was 24,109 drams ($50) per month, and the general poverty line was 41,698 drams ($87).  The law provides for a 40-hour workweek, 20 days of mandatory annual leave, and compensation for overtime and nighttime work. The law prohibits compulsory overtime in excess of four hours on two consecutive days and limits it to 180 hours in a year. The government established occupational and health standards by decree.

Authorities did not effectively enforce labor standards in either the formal or the informal sectors. The State Health Inspectorate, which employed 60 contract labor inspectors, is responsible for overseeing implementation of labor legislation and occupational safety and health standards. Resources, inspections, and remediation were inadequate, and penalties for violations of labor standards were insufficient to deter violations.

Many employees of private companies, particularly in the service and retail sectors, were unable to obtain paid leave and were required to work more than eight hours a day without additional compensation. According to representatives of some employment agencies, many employers also hired employees for an unpaid and undocumented "probationary" period of 10 to 30 days. Often employers subsequently dismissed these employees, who were then unable to claim payment for the time they worked because their initial employment was undocumented. Managers of enterprises that were the primary employers in certain poor geographic areas frequently took advantage of the absence of alternative jobs and neglected problems related to adequate pay, job safety, and environmental concerns. Nearly half of all workers found employment in the informal sector where they were vulnerable to employer abuse and without governmental protection.

Safety and health conditions remained substandard in numerous sectors, and there were several fatal workplace incidents during the year. Several cases of explosions at natural gas pumping stations and accidents at mines and construction sites led to fatalities and serious injuries due to lax safety standards and enforcement in the industry. After the accidents, the government announced it had increased the safety oversight and inspections at the natural gas filling stations. In light of high unemployment in the country, workers generally did not remove themselves from situations that endangered their health or safety. Authorities offered no protection to employees in this situation, and employees generally did not report violations of their rights.